BRIDGE
CARD BY CARD

BRIDGE
CARD BY CARD

TERENCE REESE &
BORIS SCHAPIRO

PHOTOGRAPHS BY MICHAEL HOLFORD

HAMLYN
LONDON · NEW YORK · SYDNEY · TORONTO

Second Impression 1971

©Terence Reese & Boris Schapiro 1969
Published by
THE HAMLYN PUBLISHING GROUP LIMITED
LONDON · NEW YORK · SYDNEY · TORONTO
Hamlyn House, Feltham, Middlesex, England
ISBN 0 600 00357 4

Printed in Spain by
Mateu Cromo, Artes Graficas, S.A. Madrid

'I am sorry I have not learned to play at cards.
It is very useful in life; it generates kindness
and consolidates society.'
DR SAMUEL JOHNSON 1709–1784

'In play there are two pleasures for your choosing;
The one is winning and the other losing.'
BYRON *Don Juan* 1788–1824

CONTENTS

The authors and publishers are greatly indebted to
The Amalgamated Playing Card Co. Ltd. for permission
to photograph the historic playing cards which are
illustrated in this book.

FOREWORD

The game we call simply 'Bridge' was known in its youth as 'Contract Bridge' and is only about 35 years old. However, games of the whist family, to which contract bridge belongs, have quite a long history. A game called 'Whisk' was played in the 17th century. By the time it reached fashionable society the name had been changed to the more decorous 'Whist'. A famous book, Hoyle's *Short Treatise on Whist*, was published in 1742; it both established the rules and offered instruction. The phrase 'according to Hoyle' still has the sense of correctness and precision.

In whist all four hands were held up – there was no 'dummy' – and the trump suit was determined by the last card dealt. Whist is still played, of course, though mostly as a communal recreation by people who do not take themselves seriously as card players and perhaps regard bridge players with a certain amount of awe. If that is true, bridge players do not make the corresponding error of looking down on whist players: they realise that whist is a most difficult game to play well.

During its heyday, which lasted for 150 years, whist was played with as much seriousness and almost as many conventions as bridge is today. Towards the end of the 19th century three important changes were introduced: the dealer was given the right to name the trump suit after looking at his hand (or he could pass the option to his partner); an opponent who reckoned to make the odd trick could double and the dealer could redouble; and the hand of the dealer's partner was exposed after the opening lead. Thus arose the concept of declarer and dummy.

This new form of the game was known as 'bridge'. The origin of the name is obscure. A pamphlet called *Biritch, or Russian Whist*, published at that time, has led to the belief that bridge was a corruption of a Russian word '*biritch*', but alas there is no such Russian word! An authority on card games, George F. Hervey, has an alternative, indeed an opposite, theory. It appears that in a Russian game called '*vint*' the scoring has a diagrammatic resemblance to a bridge. When the game reached England it may have been called 'the bridge game'. Then someone knowing its Russian origin may have invented the Russian-sounding word 'biritch' and attached it to his pamphlet.

What is more certain is that the game was introduced to England in 1894 by Lord Brougham, whose other contributions to civilised life included the carriage that bears his name and the development of of the French Riviera as a resort for the English.

Inevitably, it was not long before the notion of 'double' and 'redouble' was extended to the procedure we now call 'bidding'. The credit belongs to those inveterate card players, the British in India. In 1908 the first official laws for Auction Bridge were promulgated. For the first time there was competitive bidding and a defined contract.

It seems odd, looking back, that twenty years should have passed before the principle of contract bridge, where to score game a player must bid game, caught on. The idea had been present for some years in the French game of '*plafond*'. After playing '*plafond*' during a cruise in 1925 the American sportsman, Harold S. Vanderbilt, introduced the game to New York and added popular features such as vulnerability and big bonuses for slams. Contract quickly superseded Auction and Auction Bridge is now extinct. There have been some changes in the scoring since the early days of Contract, but the form of the game has not altered. Card players tend to remain conservative.

INTRODUCTION

Although the first part of this book is written for beginners, it is not just a beginner's book. We have not treated the game in a superficial way, representing it as much easier than it is. Any reader who has talent will have a chance to develop it.

The beginner will want to know how soon he may expect to be proficient. It must be admitted that bridge is not the easiest of games to learn from scratch. A game like chess, though it may give rise to most complex problems, is easy to pick up. Bridge is not like that, apart from technical knowledge, experience counts; there are no infant prodigies at this game. But do not worry, it can be fun to learn.

What qualities of mind are needed to become a good player? That is difficult to answer without begging the question. It is no use listing such qualities as a good memory or a sharp mathematical sense. Memory does not play an important part in bridge and mathematical ability is useless by itself. It is true that most expert players have good brains, but some very clever people are hopeless at cards. In the end it comes down to card sense, which is as real and indivisible as a sense of humour or a sense of direction. Some people have a natural card sense, but the important thing is that the faculty can be acquired or at least developed.

Certainly it is worth anyone's time to become a useful bridge player. Apart from the intellectual satisfaction, he will have a hobby that never palls and a means of making friends wherever he goes and in whatever society he moves. In the distant days when the present authors were schoolboys, playing cards was regarded as a minor misdemeanour, like smoking. Nowadays teams from several hundred schools enter for the annual competition organised by the English Bridge Union and the number increases every year, which is very encouraging, for bridge is first-class mental exercise and teaches more about life than Latin verbs.

It is sometimes said that bridge brings out the worst in people. It would be fairer to say that it brings out the truth. Some apparently amiable people may show themselves at the card table to be bad-tempered, greedy and vain; but equally there are opportunities for the display of such virtues as self-control, modesty and generosity.

The attractions of the game are easier to observe than to explain. For the busy person it is a perfect relaxation, for the person who has leisure it is a pastime that can be enjoyed every day of the year, for the keen and ambitious there is a path of achievement that leads eventually to the world championship. You can put into bridge, and take out, so many good things.

PART ONE
MAKING A START

MEET THE PACK

When idiomatic bridge terms occur for the first time they are printed in capital letters.

Card players do not as a rule cut their eye-teeth on bridge, so the odds are that you already know what an ordinary pack of cards looks like. There are the four suits:

Spades, denoted by the symbol   ♠

Hearts, denoted by the symbol   ♥

Diamonds, denoted by the symbol ♦

Clubs, denoted by the symbol   ♣

And there are thirteen cards in each suit:

Ace, which ranks high in bridge

King, ranking second to the Ace

Queen

Jack, also called Knave

Ten

These five are HONOURS. They are followed in rank by the plain cards:

9, 8, 7, 6, 5, 4, 3, 2

There is a ranking order of suits as well as of cards. The order is that shown above—spades, hearts, diamonds, clubs. Spades and hearts are MAJOR SUITS. Diamonds and clubs are MINOR SUITS.

Bridge is a game for four players, with two partners on each side.

The first step, unless the pairings are pre-arranged, is to draw for partners. A pack is spread out face downwards and each player draws a card. The players who have drawn the two highest cards are partners against the other two. The cards rank, remember, from the Ace to the 2. The suits matter at this stage only if two cards of the same rank are drawn. For example, suppose that these four cards are turned up:

9 of clubs
King of hearts
9 of hearts
7 of spades

The players who have cut the King of hearts and the 9 of hearts play together, as the 9 of hearts ranks higher than the 9 of clubs. This side also has the choice of seats and cards; it is usual to play with two packs of cards alternately.

In all bridge literature the four players are described as North, South, East and West; each player sitting directly opposite his partner. They occupy the positions shown in *Fig 1* in every diagram.

The player who drew the highest card, the King of hearts, deals the first hand. If he is sitting South the player on his left, West, shuffles the chosen pack and passes it across for East to CUT. This means, divide the pack into two parts, leaving it for the dealer to complete the cut. Meanwhile, the other pack is shuffled by North and placed on his right.

South deals thirteen cards, one at a time, to each player, starting with West. If he has not made a muddle, the last card will fall to himself. When the deal has been completed all the players pick up their cards and sort them into suits.

16

TRICKS & TRUMPS

There are two main stages, or 'periods', in every hand of bridge. First comes the BIDDING, then the PLAY. Here a minor embarrassment arises: you will not understand the bidding until we have told you something about the play. So we must begin at the end.

During the play each player in turn lays a card face upwards on the table. The four cards so played constitute a TRICK, and as each player began with thirteen cards there are thirteen tricks. The trick is won by the player who has contributed the best card and the general object of the game is to win as many tricks as possible.

You note that we say the trick is won by the *best* card, not the *highest* card as you will so far understand it. This is because of certain conditions in the play. The first card played to every trick is the LEAD and (with one exception that we will meet in a moment) only a card of the suit led has power to win the trick. Furthermore, each player has the unalterable duty to FOLLOW SUIT if he can. If a heart is led and you hold a heart among your cards you must play one. (If you inadvertently fail to do so you are said to REVOKE and incur a heavy penalty). Let us look at a couple of imaginary tricks:

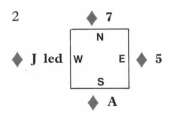

West leads the Jack of diamonds, North plays next, and everyone follows suit. No problem, the trick is won by South, who has played the highest diamond. The trick is gathered by North and placed face downwards. Later tricks won by the same side are laid across the first. As South has won the present trick he leads to the next trick as you will see illustrated below in *Fig. 3*.

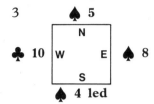

South leads the 4 of spades and West, who has no spades, DISCARDS the 10 of clubs. This discard has no power to win the trick, which in fact is taken by East's 8.

There is one important exception to the principle that a trick is won by the highest card in the suit originally led. Most hands are played with one suit as TRUMPS. The word is a corruption of 'triumph' and any card of the trump suit 'triumphs' over any card of a SIDE SUIT. In *Fig. 4* diamonds are trumps:

North leads the Queen of spades and East follows with the King. So far it is East's trick, but South, holding no spades, trumps (an alternative word is RUFFS) with the 7 of diamonds. West also has no spades and if he had a higher trump than the 7 he might OVERRUFF and win the trick from South. Instead, he discards the 10 of hearts.

You will appreciate that it is an advantage to hold several cards of the trump suit. It is not too soon for you to follow the play of a complete deal played with hearts as trumps, as shown in *Fig. 5*.

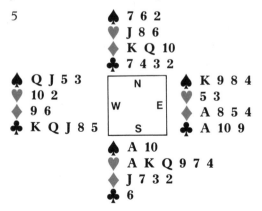

One point that has not been mentioned so far is that after the first card has been led one of the four hands is exposed on the table. This is the DUMMY. Dummy's cards are played by his partner, the DECLARER, and the opponents are the DEFENDERS.

On this hand South is the declarer. West makes the OPENING LEAD, choosing the King of clubs. North, the dummy, then lays down his cards, sorted into suits, placing the trumps on the right. Thereafter he takes no part in the play but has certain rights; for example, he may warn his partner against committing an irregularity such as revoking or leading from the wrong hand.

When the King of clubs wins the first trick West plays another club to his partner's Ace. If the hand were being played with no trump suit South would have to suffer while the defence made five tricks in clubs and one in diamonds. As it is, he is able to ruff the second club with the 4 of hearts, winning the trick. The next move is to DRAW trumps, for clearly it would be unwise to allow the enemy to win tricks by ruffing with low hearts. Thus the play goes:

Tricks 1—2 Two rounds of clubs, South ruffing the second.

Tricks 3–4 Ace and King of hearts. When both opponents follow to two rounds South knows that all the trumps have been drawn. He can see nine hearts in his own hand and dummy's, and the opponents have played four, making the necessary total of thirteen. In a common situation like this the declarer scarcely needs to count the cards: it is as simple as knowing that two and two make four.

Trick 5 A low diamond to the King and Ace. Having drawn trumps the declarer sets out to ESTABLISH tricks in diamonds. The first round is won by East's Ace.

Trick 6 East leads a spade and the Ace wins. Knowing that there are no tricks to be won in clubs, as South has no clubs and will ruff, East attacks spades, hoping to find his partner with the Ace. But South holds this card and plays it.

Tricks 7–8 The Queen and 10 of diamonds are CASHED.

Trick 9 A club is ruffed with the 7 of hearts.

South's last four cards are the Jack of diamonds, the Queen and 9 of hearts, and the 10 of spades, which is a loser. At this point he will probably lay down his cards, conceding a spade and claiming the remainder. He has made ten tricks in all, losing one club, one diamond and one spade. Not many hands are as easy to play as this one.

THE BIDDING

In the bidding, which precedes the play, the partners on each side attempt to arrive at a CONTRACT that suits the combined hands. On the deal we have just been playing, North-South made ten tricks in hearts and would score most points if they contracted to make exactly that number. When naming a contract a player does not state the full number of tricks he proposes to make but the number of ODD tricks—that is to say, the number above six. A bid of One Diamond is in theory an undertaking to make seven tricks with diamonds as trumps. A player who bid Four Hearts would be contracting to make ten tricks in hearts.

The players CALL in turn, starting with the dealer, and any contract to make a given number of tricks must overbid the existing contract. If an opponent bids Two Spades and you want to overcall him in hearts you must bid at least Three Hearts. There is a further type of bid—NO-TRUMPS. This, as you would expect, is a contract played with no suit as trumps. No-trumps ranks above all the suits, so that a bid of 2NT would outbid Two Spades.

There are three other calls that are not a contract to win a specified number of tricks and do not affect the level of the bidding. These are:
PASS, usually expressed by the words 'No BID'.
DOUBLE, meaning that you reckon to defeat an opponent's contract.
REDOUBLE, which means that, having been doubled, you express confidence in your ability to make the contract.

Here is a specimen AUCTION that shows how bidding is conducted:

South	West	North	East
No[1]	1♥[2]	2♦[3]	2♥[4]
3♦[5]	4♥[6]	5♦[7]	No[8]
No[9]	dble[10]	No[11]	No
No			

[1] TO OPEN the bidding, a player generally needs to have better than an average hand. Lacking such values, South passes. Occasionally no

player is willing to open; the hand is then PASSED OUT, or THROWN IN, and the deal passes to the next player as usual.

²West, holding above average values and a suit of hearts, opens the proceedings with One Heart.

³North, holding a suit of diamonds, contests with Two Diamonds.

⁴East, knowing that his partner holds hearts, RAISES this suit slightly.

⁵South has passed originally but comes in now with a raise of his partner's diamonds.

⁶West, having been supported by his partner, contracts for GAME in hearts. To make ten tricks in a major suit carries a special bonus.

⁷Five Diamonds, a contract to make eleven tricks in a minor, is also a game contract. However, it may well be that North is bidding Five Diamonds not in the expectation of making it but as a SACRIFICE against Four Hearts. He reckons that the PENALTY he will incur if he does not make Five Diamonds will be less than the points his opponents would score for making game in hearts.

⁸East leaves the decision to his partner. In theory, his side might pass Five Diamonds but the natural expectancy is that East-West, who have opened the bidding, will either double Five Diamonds or go to Five Hearts.

⁹South naturally has no more to say.

¹⁰If West thought he could make Five Hearts and was unlikely to defeat Five Diamonds by more than one or two tricks he might bid on. Instead, he settles for a penalty.

¹¹Either North or South could in theory redouble, but they do not because they do not expect to make Five Diamonds.

The auction ends when three players have passed the last call. North is the declarer, not because he made the final bid but because he was the first to introduce diamonds. East makes the opening lead and South puts down his dummy. If North makes, say, nine tricks he is 'two down doubled'. Finally, an auction featuring a redouble:

South	West	North	East
No	No	1♠	1NT
No	2NT	No	3NT
dble	No	No	redble
No	No	No	

Only nine tricks are needed for game at no-trumps and East-West contract for game after North has opened the bidding. South, relying on his partner's opening bid, thinks the opponents have overreached themselves and doubles. He may have misjudged the situation, for players in THIRD HAND (as North was here) sometimes open with less than the standard requirements. East is sufficiently confident to redouble. It will be an expensive hand for somebody.

OUTLINE OF THE SCORING

We	They

A score-sheet for bridge has two columns and a heavy line across the middle, as you can see from the illustration shown left.

A player enters the score for his own side in the left-hand column, the score of his opponents in the right-hand column. It is advisable for everyone to keep a separate score, for the state of the game has a profound effect on the bidding.

Full details of the scoring are shown in the table at the end of the book (page 82). Scoring soon becomes automatic, for the same scores are constantly recurring. It is not necessary for a learner to master all the scoring in advance and in this section we concentrate on the important features—not the figures themselves but the tactical objectives.

Bidding to part score, game and slam
There are three types of contract. When your side narrowly holds the balance of strength you aim to make a PART SCORE. When you hold considerable strength in some DENOMINATION (either no-trumps or a suit) you aim to make a game. Where you aspire to make twelve or thirteen tricks you may contract for a SLAM.

Most of the time, the main objective will be to score a game. Two games win the RUBBER and this carries a substantial bonus. To make a game you need to register 100 points BELOW THE LINE. The following are game contracts, assuming you have no part score from a previous hand:

THREE NO-TRUMPS	The first trick at no-trumps counts 40, each subsequent trick 30
FOUR SPADES or FOUR HEARTS	Each trick in a major suit counts 30
FIVE DIAMONDS or FIVE CLUBS	Each trick in a minor suit counts 20

Game can be made in two or more stages, so it is essential to record the exact value of any part score you may make. Say that on the first hand of a rubber you bid Two Diamonds and make Three (i.e. nine tricks). You enter 40 below the line, as your contract was for Two Diamonds only, and the OVERTRICK, also worth 20, is scored ABOVE THE LINE. Having 40 below you need to make 2NT or Two of a major or Three of a minor to score game. When you have made a game you draw a line beneath it and this line cancels out any part scores made by either side in so far as they contribute to the next game. Ignoring, for the present, any penalties above the line in respect of contracts not made, a specimen rubber might go like this:

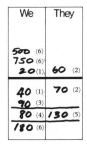

We	They
500 (6)	
750 (6)	
20 (1)	**60** (2)
40 (1)	**70** (2)
90 (3)	
80 (4)	**130** (5)
180 (6)	

Deal 1 You bid Two Diamonds and make Three, scoring 40 below and 20 above.

Deal 2 Your opponents bid 2NT and make ten tricks. It seems as though they have underestimated their hands. At any rate, they do not score game. They score 70 below (40+30) and 60 above for the two overtricks.

Deal 3 You bid Two Hearts and make Three. Strictly speaking, this should be entered as 60 below and 30 above, but as you have scored game it is normal practice to write the full score in one place.

Deal 4 You begin the new game by bidding Four Clubs and just making it. This gives you 80 below the line.

Deal 5 Opponents bid 3NT and make Four. As they have bid game the total score of 130 may be entered below as a single figure. This game 'kills' your part score of 80.

Deal 6 Happy omen, you bid a slam, Six Spades, and make it. A successful contract for twelve tricks is a SMALL SLAM, a contract for thirteen tricks, quite rare, a GRAND SLAM. You would score a bonus of 750 for the small slam and also 500 for winning the rubber in three games. Here, again, you could write the total of 1430 in one place. At the end of the rubber the scores are added up.

Penalties and vulnerability
Whenever you fail to make a contract you incur a penalty. These points are scored above the line. A side that has scored a game is said to be VULNERABLE and the penalties are higher than when not vulnerable. The slam bonuses and the rewards for making overtricks in a doubled contract are also higher.

The effect of a double or redouble

When a contract is doubled the tricks score is multiplied by two, and when it is redoubled, by four. If you are doubled in Two Spades and make it you score 120 below and have been DOUBLED INTO GAME. There is a bonus of 50 for making any doubled or redoubled contract and overtricks are well rewarded. By the same token, penalties are much increased. As an example, three down undoubled, not vulnerable, costs 150, but three down doubled is 500.

Bonus for honours

Any player, whether a declarer or defender, who holds four or five honours in the trump suit, or four aces at no-trumps, scores a bonus. The points scored are inconsiderable and have, or should have, only a marginal effect on the choice of contract. An 'honours hog' costs himself and his partners thousands of points in a year.

Realities of the score-sheet

The scoring at bridge is deceptive in some ways. Often there is a 'hidden value', not written down on the score-sheet. As a simple example, no bonus is directly scored for the first game made by either side, but the first game is nearly as valuable as the second. Even at this early stage of your bridge career it is well to understand the realities that underlie the scoring:

Whether vulnerable or not, you are entitled to go for a game which is *slightly* against the odds; but do not despise the tactical value of a part score.

Whether vulnerable or not, you are entitled to bid a small slam on an even chance.

On the other hand, you need heavy odds in favour before you abandon a safe small slam for a grand slam.

The odds are loaded against the doubler. Do not double any contract unless you have good grounds for supposing you can defeat it.

In general, it pays to go two down doubled as a sacrifice against a game contract, but three down shows a slight loss whatever the vulnerability.

PART TWO
HOW TO BID

WHAT IS YOUR HAND WORTH?

By now you know how bridge is played and are ready to pass on, probably with some relief, to the problem of how to play it well.

If you have listened to bridge players discussing hands you will have heard them say, 'I had so-many points'. Almost all players nowadays value their hands initially in terms of a POINT COUNT. This measures the value of high cards as follows:

Ace   =4 points
King   =3 points
Queen =2 points
Jack   =1 point

Look again at the South hand in *Fig. 5* on page 20:

6 ♠ A 10
  ♥ A K Q 9 7 4
  ♦ J 7 3 2
  ♣ 6

This hand contains 14 high-card points, an Ace above average. It also contains a good heart suit. The 6-4-2-1 DISTRIBUTION is a further asset. Some systems of valuation assign additional points to 'shape'. However, you cannot play bridge by numbers and the way to sum up this hand is '14 points, a good major suit and good distribution'.

7 ♠ K 9 8 4
  ♥ 5 3
  ♦ A 8 5 4
  ♣ A 10 9

Now look at *Fig. 7*, which is East's hand in the same diagram: this hand contains 11 points, one above average. It has no good distributional features, but at least 4-4-3-2 is potentially better than a flat 4-3-3-3. Also the hand contains fair INTERMEDIATES. The 9 and 8 of spades and the 10 and 9 of clubs may prove useful, especially if the contract is no-trumps.

Fig. 8 shows a third type of hand. This is a TWO-SUITER. It contains 12 points but more significant are the two good suits. The value of this type of hand depends very much on the FIT with partner. If he has good support for either of your suits you are well away; but if he has a 'black' hand, composed mostly of spades and clubs, the problem will be not to get too high.

Next, there is the PRE-EMPTIVE type (*Fig. 9*), a one-suiter with good playing strength but few high cards.

Only 7 points but a fair hand in terms of playing tricks. With this type, as we will see later, it is normal to bid high in spades at the first opportunity.

What we want you to understand at this stage is that there are two elements of strength in any bridge hand—high cards and distribution. Both elements are taken into account when you decide whether to open the bidding.

WHEN TO OPEN THE BIDDING

Opening bids conform to long established and soundly based conventions. There are six types of opening, which we will discuss in turn. They are:

a Opening bids of One of a suit.   *d* Opening bids of 1NT and 2NT.

b Opening bids of Two of a suit.   *e* Opening bids of Three and Four.
(not clubs).

c Opening bid of Two Clubs.   *f* Opening bid of 3NT.

(a) Opening bids of One of a suit

About four-fifths of all opening bids are of One of a suit. As you will deduce from that, the range is wide, from about 11 to 20 points. *Figs. 10* and *11* are examples.

```
10   ♠ A Q J 9 7 5      11   ♠ K Q J 8 4
     ♥ 5                     ♥ A J 10 7 6
     ♦ K J 8 3                ♦ 7
     ♣ 4 2                    ♣ 8 5
```

These hands contain only 11 points but are strongly distributed. The first has a good spade suit and 6-4-2-1 shape, the second is a major two-suiter. Either would be a sound opening in any position at the table (i.e. whether in first, second, third or fourth position) and at any vulnerability. On both hands you open One Spade.

```
12   ♠ 6 2             13   ♠ A Q 6 4
     ♥ K Q 8 5 3            ♥ 5 3
     ♦ A J 8 3             ♦ J 8 6
     ♣ Q 6                 ♣ K Q 8 5
```

These are minimum 12-point hands. On (*12*) you open One Heart, naturally. On (*13*) it is safer to open One Club, a low bid leaving plenty of space, than One Spade.

14 ♠ J 8 3 2   15 ♠ K Q 6 2
    ♥ K 10 7   ♥ 6
    ♦ K 8 4   ♦ A J 9 7
    ♣ A Q 6   ♣ K 6 5 2

Fig. 14 is a characterless 13-pointer. If one of the Kings were a Queen we would advise a pass. It is normal to open with 13 points, but what shall we open? The hand is not strong enough for 1NT (see below) and the only four-card suit is very weak. On such hands it is best to open with an APPROACH BID of One Club. Do not be afraid to introduce a three-card minor, you will not be left to play there; but do not bid weak major suits on weak hands.

Fig. 15 shows a moderate three-suiter. The best opening is One Diamond, leaving room for partner to respond One Heart.

16 ♠ A Q 6   17 ♠ 6
    ♥ 8 4   ♥ A K J 7 2
    ♦ A K J 6   ♦ A 8
    ♣ A Q 7 3   ♣ A Q 10 8 4

The two hands shown in *Figs. 16* and *17* are close to maximum One bids. The first totals 20 points but has no long suit and an opening of One Diamond is sufficient. The second hand is more powerful but lacks the solidity for a Two bid. Open One Heart and hope you will have an opportunity to show the clubs. As we will see in a later section, partner will respond to a bid of One on quite moderate values.

(b) Opening bids of Two of a suit (not clubs)

Some hands are so powerful that you feel you must make sure of a second chance. True, you could open with a bid that would give you game, but you might arrive at the wrong contract. For example, you pick up as shown in *Fig. 18*:

18 ♠ A Q J 9 8 7
    ♥ A K J 8 4
    ♦ K 5
    ♣ none

You need only a moderate fit to be sure of game but it might prove a mistake to open, say, Four Spades. Partner might hold a SINGLETON (one card) or VOID (no cards) in spades and have support for hearts. The solution is to open Two Spades. This bid is FORCING for one round. If partner is weak—less than about 8 points—he will make the NEGATIVE response of 2NT. Then you will introduce your hearts.

Figs. 19 and *20* are further hands on which you would open with a Two bid.

19   ♠ 6
    ♥ A K J 9 8 7 5
    ♦ A Q 8
    ♣ K 4

20   ♠ A K Q 8 6 4 2
    ♥ K 5
    ♦ A Q J
    ♣ 10

On *Fig. 19* open Two Hearts and rebid simply Three Hearts over the weakness response of 2NT. You must not twist your partner's arm any further. On *Fig. 20* open Two Spades and rebid Four Spades, for now you have at least nine probable tricks in your own hand. The spades look solid for seven tricks, you must make at least two diamonds and the King of hearts is a further asset.

(c) Opening Two Clubs

Now you meet for the first time an ARTIFICIAL CONVENTION. An opening bid of Two Clubs bears no relation to clubs and is a way of saying, 'I practically have game in my own hand and I want you to keep the bidding open until game is reached, except for one sequence'. Most hands worth a Two Club opening add up to 20 points or more but there is no fixed requirement. With a weak hand partner will give you the negative response of Two Diamonds. Any other response is POSITIVE and promises about an Ace and King or two King-Queens or the equivalent in high cards.

21   ♠ A 8
    ♥ A K J 9 4
    ♦ A K Q 8 4
    ♣ Q

22   ♠ A Q 7
    ♥ K Q 10 8
    ♦ A K 9
    ♣ A Q 6

On *Fig. 21* open Two Clubs and over a negative response of Two Diamonds bid simply Two Hearts. There is no need to jump either now or later, for partner is obliged to keep the bidding open until game is reached. On the second hand (*22*) a BALANCED 24 points, rebid 2NT over Two Diamonds. This particular sequence is usually played as non-forcing, though responder needs only about 3 points to raise to game.

It must be added that the artificial Two Clubs is a SYSTEM bid, not universally accepted. When you face an unfamiliar partner it is usual to ask about systems. If he doesn't appear to have heard of the artificial Two Clubs, then forget it!

(d) Opening bids of 1NT and 2NT

There are different theories about the best range for an opening 1NT. Without going into the various fashions we advise a medium no-trump of 15–17 points, irrespective of vulnerability. The hand should be fairly balanced and certainly should not contain a singleton.

	23			24	
	♠	K J 7		♠	10 5 4
	♥	A Q 8		♥	A 9
	♦	K 10 8 5		♦	A Q 8
	♣	Q J 6		♣	K Q 10 7 3

The first hand, a 4-3-3-3 16 points, is dead centre for 1NT. On the second hand an opening One Club would not be a mistake, but 1NT is at least as good.

There is a gap between a maximum 1NT and a minimum 2NT. The range for 2NT is 20–22.

	25			26	
	♠	K J 4		♠	K 7
	♥	A K 8 3		♥	A J 3
	♦	K Q 7		♦	A K Q 10 8
	♣	A J 8		♣	Q J 5

Fig. 25 is an orthodox 2NT opening and on *Fig. 26* 2NT is tactically superior to One Diamond or Two Diamonds.

(e) Opening bids of Three and Four

As there is ample machinery at the Two level for all types of strong hand, opening bids above that level are *pre-emptive* in character. The word means 'buy before' and when you pre-empt you aim to buy the contract before the opponents have had time to get together. You do this when you hold a long suit and less in high cards than would be expected from an opening bid of One.

	27			28	
	♠	6		♠	7 6
	♥	K J 10 9 7 6 2		♥	8 2
	♦	J 10 4		♦	A J 10 9 8 7 4 2
	♣	8 3		♣	5

Fig. 27 is not too weak a hand for a non-vulnerable Three Hearts. Do not worry that if partner has nothing you may end with about five tricks and be four down doubled. In that case the opponents would have enough for a slam and you would be doing well to get out for a penalty of 700. On the second hand *Fig. 28* you might open Four Diamonds if not vulnerable, Three Diamonds if vulnerable.

Pack of Astronomy Cards with Original Slipcase

AUTUMNUS

COURT GAME
OF
ASTRONOMY

PEGASUS

AQUARIUS   PISCES

CYGNUS

GLORIA FREDERICI   ANDROMEDA

JUPITER

ARGO NAVIS

HYDRA   MONOCEROS

ANTLIA
PNEUMATICA   CANIS MAJOR

PYXIS
NAUTICA

PISCIS VOLANS

MARS

AURIGA

LYNX   CAMELOPARDALIS

PERSEUS   TRIANGULUM

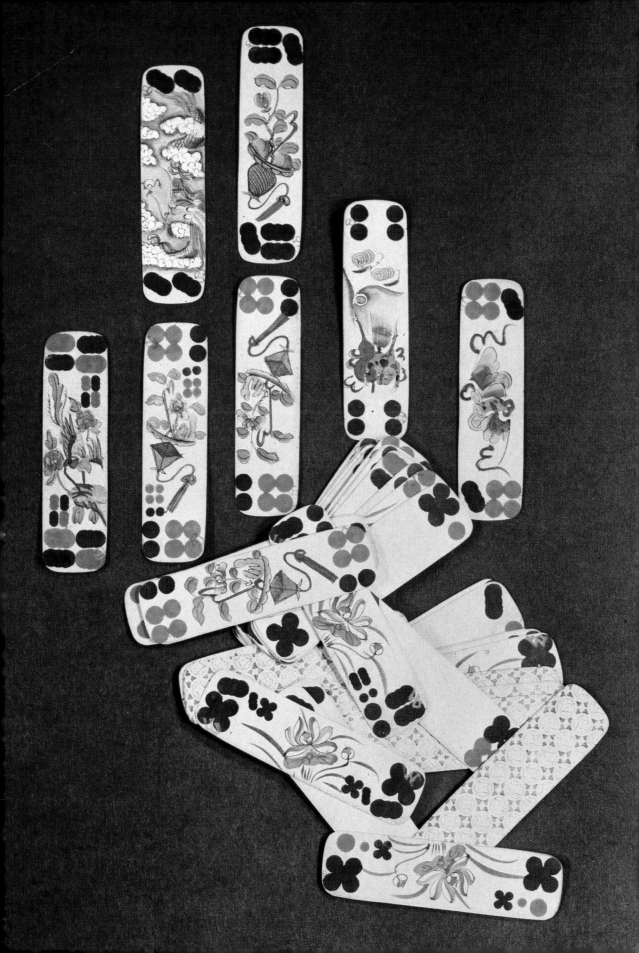

(f) Opening 3NT

An opening bid of 3NT is a special case. Playing a Two Club system you would open Two Clubs on a very strong balanced hand. Clearly it would be uneconomical to use 3NT for the same purpose. The bid is commonly made on hands containing a long and solid minor suit, often with no strength outside. If partner does not fancy the prospects in no-trumps he can take out into Four Clubs. Played in this fashion, 3NT is a semi-pre-emptive opening; naturally it is advisable to make sure that partner is on the same wavelength.

RESPONSE TO AN OPENING SUIT BID OF ONE

The first response to partner's suit opening is perhaps the most critical bid in the game. We examine it under six headings:

a Denial bid	Pass
b Limited bids	1NT or a single raise
c Bids of variable strength	Simple change of suit
d Invitations to game	2NT or double raise
e Game-going bids	3NT or a raise to game
f Bids of unlimited strength	Jump in a new suit.

(a) Denial bid – Pass

An opening bid of One may be quite strong, as we have seen, but it is still advisable to pass on a moderate hand of not more than 6 points, especially if there is no suit that can be bid at the range of One. Partner has opened One Spade and you hold hands *29* and *30*.

29	♠ 8 4 2	30	♠ 5
	♥ Q 6 3		♥ Q 10 8 7 4 2
	♦ K 5 4 2		♦ Q 7 4 3
	♣ J 6 3		♣ 6 2

On *Fig. 29* you have a featureless 6 points with no Ace and no intermediates. Game could be on if partner had a maximum but on the balance of probabilities you should pass.

Fig. 30 presents an uncomfortable decision for two reasons: you have a singleton spade and there is probably a better contract available; secondly, if partner is strong and has support for hearts there could be a game in that suit. Here, again, it is unwise to look on the bright side only. To pass is less dangerous than to bid either 1NT or Two Hearts. It is by no means unlikely that FOURTH HAND (the last player to speak) will re-open the bidding and give you a chance to express your hand more accurately.

(b) Limited bids – 1NT or a single raise

A response of 1NT is quite weak, signifying about 7 to 9 points and denying the ability to make any more constructive or informative call. Respond 1NT to One Heart on either of hands *31* or *32*.

31 ♠ Q 7 6
♥ Q 4
♦ K 8 6 2
♣ J 10 8 4

32 ♠ K 7 3
♥ 6
♦ K 8 7 4 2
♣ J 6 3 2

Fig. 32 contains a five-card suit but 1NT, limiting the values, is sounder than Two Diamonds.

A single raise shows a moderate hand with support for partner's suit. Again partner has opened One Heart and you hold hands as shown in *Figs. 33* and *34*.

33 ♠ 7 2
♥ K J 8
♦ 10 6 4 3 2
♣ Q 8 3

34 ♠ 10 8 4
♥ J 7 6 4 2
♦ 3
♣ Q 6 5 3

On *Fig. 33* you hold only three trumps, but they are good ones and you have a DOUBLETON (two cards) in a side suit. This is a weak raise to Two Hearts. Hand *34* is an example of a distributional raise. You hold only 3 points, but no matter, the five trumps and the singleton represent useful support.

(c) Bids of variable strength – Simple change of suit

A response at the level of One in a new suit has a wide range. It may be a modest 5 points with a fair suit or it may go up to about 15 points. Partner has opened One Diamond and you hold hands *35* and *36*.

35 ♠ K J 8 7 4
♥ J 9
♦ 6 2
♣ 10 8 5 2

36 ♠ A K 7 3
♥ K Q 7
♦ 10 3
♣ Q 8 4 2

On either hand respond One Spade. You certainly have game values on hand *36* and a jump to Two Spades would not be a mistake. However, it is slightly under strength for this jump and you can be sure of a second chance, for this is the moment to mention a very important principle in bidding: A CHANGE OF SUIT BY RESPONDER IS FORCING FOR ONE ROUND. It is the opener's duty to make one further call even when he is minimum. (This does not apply when the responder has passed originally.)

A response at the range of Two is more encouraging. The minimum with only a fair suit is about 9 points. With a strong rebiddable suit you may make the response on 7 or 8. Partner has opened One Heart and you hold hands as shown in *Figs. 37* and *38*.

37	♠	7 4		38	♠	K 4
	♥	Q 5			♥	5
	♦	A J 8 6 3			♦	K J 10 9 7 6
	♣	Q 7 4 2			♣	6 4 3 2

Hand *37* is about a minimum for a response at the Two level with an average suit. On *Fig. 38* you may respond Two Diamonds because the suit is strong enough to repeat. For example, if the bidding begins One Heart–Two Diamonds–2NT you will SIGN OFF in Three Diamonds, warning partner that you are short of high cards and do not fancy the prospects of game in no-trumps.

(d) Invitations to game - 2NT or a double raise

When your partner has opened the bidding and you hold 11–12 points you may reckon that you are close to game. On a balanced hand you express this with a response of 2NT. With *Fig. 39* respond 2NT over any opening.

39	♠	A 10 4
	♥	Q 9 3
	♦	K 8 5 2
	♣	K 8 6

If the opening bid were One Diamond you would have the values for a raise to Three, but 2NT gives a better picture of the all-round strength. This response is not forcing but partner will pass only on a minimum.

A double raise is likewise a strong invitation to game. Four trumps are necessary. *Figs. 40* and *41* show typical hands for a raise of One Spade to Three Spades.

40	♠	K 10 8 4		41	♠	Q 10 8 5 2
	♥	Q 5			♥	8
	♦	A K 7 4			♦	Q J 2
	♣	Q 8 5			♣	K 9 6 3

(e) Game-going bids - 3NT or a raise to game

A response of 3NT suggests a balanced 14–16. A 13-point hand is on the borderline between 2NT and 3NT; you will be guided by the intermediate cards.

A raise to game in either a major or a minor tends to be based mainly on distributional values. Compare hands *42* and *43*.

On *Fig. 42* it would not be a mistake to raise One Spade to Four Spades, but this might lead to a missed slam. It is better to respond Two Diamonds for the moment and raise spades on the next round. Hand *43* is a more typical raise of One Spade to Four Spades. In the same way you would raise One Club to Four or even Five Clubs.

(f) Bids of unlimited strength - a jump in a new suit

When your hand is too strong for any of the treatments described so far, you FORCE TO GAME by jumping in a new suit. With a strong suit of your own or with strong support for partner you may force on about 14 points; lacking any special feature, the usual minimum is 16. Partner has opened One Heart and you hold hands *44* and *45*.

```
44  ♠ A 8              45  ♠ A Q J 10 4 2
    ♥ K J 10 6              ♥ 7 2
    ♦ K 9 6 5               ♦ A K 8
    ♣ A 10 3               ♣ J 6
```

Hand *44* is too strong for a direct raise to Four Hearts and Two Diamonds followed by a raise to game would also be insufficient. The answer is to force with Three Diamonds (or Three Clubs). When on the next round you proceed to Four Hearts partner will know you are very strong. On hand *45* it is true that a response of One Spade would be forcing for one round but it is better to get the hand off your chest with a game force of Two Spades. You save time in the end because if you did not jump now you would have to bid at least Four Spades on the next round. Once you have forced with Two Spades you can go slowly, for remember that after this type of response neither partner may drop the bidding short of game.

BIDDING TO GAME & SLAM

After the opening bid and response the developments are so numerous that one must deal in general advice rather than particular examples. We do this under the following headings:

a Reaching game in no-trumps
b Reaching game in a suit
c The way to slam

(a) Reaching game in no-trumps

When you know that the partnership contains a minimum of 25 points you may expect to have a play for game in no-trumps. With a long suit you will often make game on less, but we are referring to hands where you have at most one or two five-card suits.

In the light of this standard, see how easy it is to calculate raises of 1NT. The opening promises 15–17 points. If you have 9 points or a barren 10 points you may raise to 2NT. With 11 or a 'good' 10 you may go to game.

Sometimes when partner has opened 1NT you will be uncertain at first whether to play for game at no-trumps or in a suit. With a five-card major suit and a singleton and upwards of 9 points you may jump to Three of the suit. This is game-forcing. A simple take-out, Two of a suit óver 1NT, should normally be passed by the opener.

When you move into the wider world of bridge you will find that many players use the STAYMAN CONVENTION, in which a response of Two Clubs to 1NT is conventional, asking the opener to name a four-card major suit if he has one. Lacking such a suit, the opener rebids Two Diamonds.

Of course you will often try for game at no-trumps after a suit opening and a suit response. Suppose the bidding begins:

South	North
1 ♦	1 ♥
2 ♦	?

South has made a limited rebid and may have only about 12 points. To suggest game at no-trumps North needs about the same as for an immediate reply of 2NT, 11–12 points.

(b) Reaching game in a suit

Suppose the bidding begins One Heart–Two Hearts or One Heart–1NT. In either case responder is strictly limited. The opener now needs about an Ace better than a minimum before he can think about game. With a fairly balanced hand he needs about 17 points to raise 1NT to 2NT.

From responder's side, this is a useful formula to remember: AN OPENING BID OPPOSITE AN OPENING BID WILL NORMALLY PRODUCE A GAME. You may apply this test in the following ways:

1 Partner has opened, you have the values for an opening bid yourself and the hands appear to fit reasonably. There should be a game somewhere.

2 Partner has opened and made a jump rebid, as in the sequences 1♥–1♠–2NT or 1♥–1♠–3♥. For this strong rebid the opener should hold about an Ace and a Jack better than minimum or compensating values in the form of a long suit. If the addition of an Ace and a Jack to your own hand would put you in the opening range you may expect a game unless there is an evident misfit. When you sense a misfit–particularly when you are void of a suit that partner has rebid–do not fight the elements. Pass before worse happens.

(c) The way to slam

About one hand in ten contains slam possibilities but you must not expect to bid all the slams or indeed more than half. If you can do that, and seldom go down in a slam you have bid, you will be doing better than most players. Here are a few tests you can apply that will help you to judge whether you are in the slam zone:

1 If you can count 33–34 points in the combined hands there will be a play for 6NT unless both hands are very balanced.

Say that the bidding begins:

South	North
1♦	1♠
3NT	?

North holds 14 points including a five-card suit. His partner's rebid of 3NT is very strong, indicating a maximum One bid of 19–20 points. North can count a minimum of 33 in the combined hands and can go direct to 6NT.

2 When one player has the values for a jump rebid and the other has the values for an opening bid, there should be a play for slam if a suitable denomination exists.

The bidding begins:

	South	North
	1♥	1♠
	3♠	?

North holds the hand as shown in *Fig. 46*.

46 ♠ K Q J 4 2
    ♥ K 5
    ♦ J 4
    ♣ A 6 3 2

Here North has an opening bid himself and his partner has opened and given a jump raise. A slam is likely but there might possibly be two quick losers in diamonds. North's next move should be a CUE-BID of Four Clubs. As spades have been CONFIRMED by the jump raise Four Clubs shows a CONTROL, not a suit. If South holds first or second round control of diamonds he will accept the slam invitation with a cue-bid in diamonds.

3 If you could take an Ace away from your hand and still be confident of game, you may investigate a slam.

This test can be applied in a great variety of situations. Say that the bidding begins:

	South	North
	1♠	2♦
	3♦	?

See *Fig. 47* for North's hand.   *Take in fig. 47*

47 ♠ K 5
    ♥ 4
    ♦ A Q J 7 3 2
    ♣ K Q 6 4

If you held a small diamond instead of the Ace you would still expect to make ten or eleven tricks in diamonds, so that is one way of judging that you must be close to slam. The danger here is that you might be missing two Aces. That brings us to the BLACKWOOD CONVENTION, of which you have possibly heard tell. Playing the convention you would now bid 4NT, asking partner to indicate how many Aces he holds. South will respond according to the following schedule:

Five Clubs	No Ace or four Aces
Five Diamonds	One Ace
Five Hearts	Two Aces
Five Spades	Three Aces

A subsequent bid of 5NT by the player who has bid a Blackwood 4NT may be used to enquire for Kings according to the same schedule.

Blackwood serves a useful purpose on this type of hand where the playing tricks are obviously there and all you need is reassurance about Aces. But do not fall into the popular error of enquiring about Aces and taking a chance on the playing tricks. Otherwise, like many an international pair before you, you will go with slams to the slaughter!

THE DEFENDING SIDE

When one side has opened, the other side are the defenders and make DEFENSIVE OVERCALLS. The minimum standards are lower than for opening bids, but strong counter-measures are also available. We discuss in turn:

a Simple overcalls

b Jump overcalls

c Take-out doubles

d Cue-bids

e Overcalls in fourth position

(a) Simple overcalls

A player who opens the bidding is laying the foundations for a constructive sequence, but a player who overcalls is often more concerned with obstruction than with buying the contract. You may think of the defenders as waging guerilla warfare. Points are no longer a guide. The main consideration is safety and the most important element is a fair suit. Before you take any risk you must be satisfied that your bid stands to gain. Compare *Figs. 48* and *49*.

	48		49
♠	A Q 10 7 4	♠	A J 7 5
♥	7 3	♥	Q 5 2
♦	Q 10 8 6	♦	Q J 6
♣	5 2	♣	10 8 6

On *Fig. 48* you have a sound One Spade overcall. On *Fig. 49* you should pass because the suit is poor and your hand is defensive in general character. Especially when vulnerable you need good playing strength for an overcall at the Two level.

	50		51
♠	A 8	♠	A 8
♥	6 4	♥	7 4 2
♦	K J 8 7 6 3	♦	K J 7 5 3
♣	K 7 2	♣	Q 7 2

The player in front of you has opened One Heart or One Spade. Hand *50* would be risky, hand *51* an extremely poor overcall.

(b) Jump overcalls

A jump overcall, Two Spades over One Diamond, Three Clubs over One Heart, is strength-showing but not forcing. Over One Club you would overcall with Two Hearts:

52 ♠ 7 3
♥ A Q J 9 7 4
♦ A K 8
♣ 6 2

(c) Take-out doubles

By far the commonest form of counter-attack by a defender who has a promising hand is a TAKE-OUT DOUBLE. By universal convention a low-level double when the doubler's partner has not bid conveys the message: 'I have a useful hand. Tell me where your strength lies'.

South opens One Diamond and West holds hand 53.

53 ♠ K 9 7 4   54 ♠ A Q J 8 4
♥ K 10 8 7 3   ♥ A 8 3
♦ 4   ♦ 6 2
♣ A J 5   ♣ K Q 6

Hand 53 is a good distributional double. It is below the standard for an opening bid but contains good support for any suit that partner may call. Hand 54 is too strong for a simple overcall and the values are too well distributed for Two Spades. Best is to double and bid spades on the next round.

The partner of the player who has doubled will normally respond in his best suit. If his only suit has been called by the opponents he may either bid no-trumps or, with exceptional length in the suit doubled, he may pass, converting the take-out double into a penalty double. One thing he must never do is pass from general weakness. With a fair hand, about 9 points upwards, he must jump to show that he is better than minimum.

It is convenient to mention at this point that take-out doubles are also available to the side that has opened the bidding.

South	West	North	East
1♠	2♣	No	No
dble			

As North has not spoken, except to pass, South's double is for take-out. It shows a strong hand, probably with a shortage in clubs. North may now introduce a red suit which he was too weak to bid on the first round, or he may revert to Two Spades or, with tricks in clubs, he may make a PENALTY PASS.

Note that the double would have an entirely different meaning if the bidding had been:

South	West	North	East
1♠	No	1NT	2♣
dble			

Here North has given some account of his hand by responding 1NT. South's double is therefore for penalties.

55	♠ A Q 9 7 3	56	♠ A K 10 3
	♥ A K 10 8 5 2		♥ A J 8 4 2
	♦ 4		♦ none
	♣ A		♣ K Q J 3

(d) Cue-bids

The strongest overcall is a bid of the opponent's suit. This is another form of cue-bid. South opens One Diamond and West holds *55*.

On *Fig. 55* the way to be sure of a chance to show your giant two-suiter is to overcall with Two Diamonds. If partner responds in clubs, as is likely, you may follow with Three Diamonds, pressing him to choose between the majors. On the second hand any response to Two Diamonds will suit you. It follows that when you are very strong in the suit opened by an opponent you must not overcall in that suit. South opens One Heart and as West you hold hand *57*.

57	♠ 5
	♥ A Q 10 8 6 3
	♦ K J 7 3
	♣ Q 2

Do not give South a contemptuous look and bid Two Hearts. The next thing you might hear would be Three or Four Spades from your partner. The only sensible action over One Heart is a TRAP PASS. Quite possibly the opponents are heading for trouble; give them a little rope.

(e) Overcalls in fourth position

When an opening bid is followed by two passes the player in fourth position should normally re-open on quite moderate values. For example, 1NT in the PROTECTIVE position suggests about 11–14 points. Do not be nervous of giving the opponents a second chance.

PART THREE
HOW TO PLAY

WAYS OF WINNING TRICKS

When you learn to play golf or tennis you begin by practising individual strokes. In the same way, at bridge, the first step is to observe ways of developing tricks in a single suit. You develop tricks by establishing low cards, by promoting high cards, and by plays that depend on finding the cards favourably placed.

Establishing low-card winners
You will have realised that bridge is not just a game of Aces and Kings. Almost as many tricks are won by low cards as by high cards. In many cases you establish low-card winners simply by playing off the top cards.

	58	**K Q 7 3**		59	**K 8 6 5 3**
		A 5 2			**A Q 7**

In the first example (*Fig. 58*) you play off the Ace, King and Queen. If everyone has followed suit the last card, the thirteenth, will be Good. There is no need to count; you will meet this type of situation so often that the calculation will be instinctive. In the second case (*Fig. 59*) you have a good chance to establish two low-card tricks. If both opponents follow to the Ace and Queen the rest of dummy's cards will be winners.

One small and, we trust, obvious point here: it would be a mistake to begin with the Ace and then play low to the King because this would leave you in the wrong hand to play off the remaining winners. In general it is right to cash high cards in the short suit first. Otherwise you may run into entry problems.

It is worth knowing also that the odds are against your finding the opposing cards divided 3–3 in the first example but in favour of finding them 3–2 in the second example. Knowledge of that sort is very important when you plan the play of an entire hand.

51

Very often you will have to surrender one or more tricks to establish low winners.

60	A K 7 5 2	61	A 8 6 4 2
	6 4		7 5 3

With the cards as in *Fig. 60* you may make four tricks if the opposing cards are divided 3–3. It will probably be sound tactics to DUCK the first round, playing low from each hand. After that, if all follow to the Ace and King, the last two cards in dummy will be good. In *Fig. 61* the normal play would be to duck twice, letting the opponents win the first two rounds. The advantage of playing in this way is that you retain a third card to lead to dummy's A 8 6.

Promoting high cards

Many tricks are won by forcing out an opponent's high cards so that your own are promoted to winning rank.

62	K Q 10	63	Q J 10 6
	J 7 3 2		9 5

The first situation (*Fig. 62*) occurred in the hand on page 20. You simply force out the Ace and then have three certain tricks. In the second example (*Fig. 63*) you promote two winners by forcing out the Ace and King.

Promotion of high cards and establishment of low cards often go together, as in *Figs. 64* and *65*.

64	K J 7 4 2	65	10 8 5 3 2
	Q 3		Q J

In the first case you lead the Queen and, if the Ace is not played, continue with a second round. If the suit is divided 3–3 you win four tricks and if it is 4–2 you may still have time to set up one LONG CARD. With *65* you need to force out the Ace and King. If all goes well you will end up with three winners; you need to find the suit 3–3 or drop the 9 in two rounds.

The positional factor

With a great many combinations it is essential to lead from the right hand, taking advantage of the positional factor in play. In the examples so far it would have made no difference, but most of the time it is necessary to lead up to honours rather than away from them. This principle appears in its purest form when we study the play known as a FINESSE.

Above left : 18th Century English Cards. *Centre left :* Cards by Grimaud of Paris. *Below left :* Cards made in Genova, Italy. *Right :* 19th Century French Cards

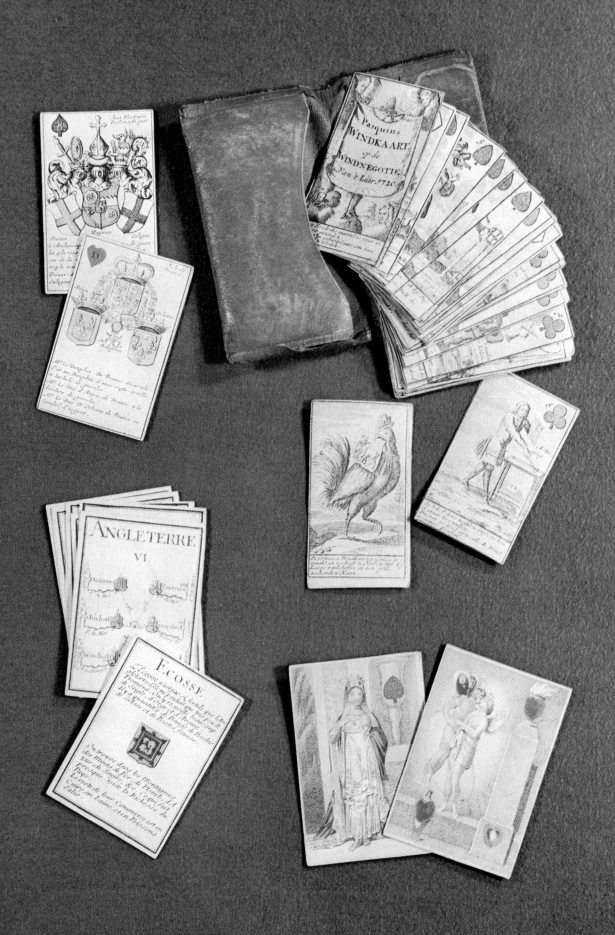

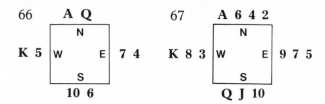

Fig. *66* illustrates the perfect finesse position. You lead the 6 from hand, West plays the 5 and you successfully finesse the Queen. It is plain that if you had led from North instead of from South you would have lost a trick to the King. With the cards as in (*67*) you lead the Queen from hand. Whether West plays the King on this trick or on a later trick you can arrive at four winners with the aid of a finesse and a 3–3 break.

Finesses against the Queen are equally common.

68 **K J 5**
    A 6 4 2

69 **A J 8**
    K 10 9

With *68* you lead low and put in the Jack, hoping that the Queen is held by West. In *Fig. 69* you have an example of a two-way finesse. You may play either opponent for the Queen. Still better, you will observe, is to let the opponents open up this suit. That is true of various holdings.

Figs. 70 and *71* are examples of a finesse against the Jack.

70 **K 7 3**
    Q 10 6 4

71 **Q 9 6 5 4**
    10 8 2

With *Fig. 70* you begin with a low card up to the King. Whether this wins or not, the next play will be a finesse of the 10. With *Fig. 71* you lead the 8 from hand and let it run if not covered. If West began with, say, K J x (the x standing for any low card) you may win three tricks in the suit eventually.

There are innumerable positions where the declarer does not take a finesse in the literal sense but makes a play that depends on the cards being favourably placed.

72 **K 6**
    7 4

73 **Q 7 5**
    A 4 2

Clearly, in *Fig. 72*, it is advisable to lead up to the King rather than away from it. In *Fig. 73* it would be a mistake to lead the Queen from dummy, for if East held the King he would cover and you would end

Above left : Brianville's Heraldry Cards. *Below left :* Cards from a 17th Century French Pack. *Above right :* Dutch Cards of the South Sea Bubble Crisis. *Below right :* 18th Century French Cards of Viennese Design

up with only one trick. The correct play is low from hand towards the Queen, gaining whenever West holds the King. Finally, the declarer will often finesse in effect against two honours.

74 **A Q 10**
     7 4 3

75 **A J 10**
     6 4 2

With the cards as in *Fig. 74* the only chance for three tricks is to start with a DOUBLE FINESSE of the 10, playing West for K J x. Example *75* presents a COMBINATION FINESSE. On the first round you finesse the 10. This will probably lose to the King or Queen. In that case you take a second finesse against the remaining honour with good chances of success. You make two tricks unless East began with K Q x.

We have touched on only a small number of the possible suit combinations. You will find it a very good exercise to extract the cards of a single suit, divide them in a number of ways, and work out the line of play that provides the best chance to win a given number of tricks.

THE PLAY AT NO-TRUMPS

Hands played in no-trumps fall into two general types. Sometimes all the hands are balanced and the general object of the defence is to make safe leads that give nothing away and leave declarer to do his own work. More often, one or both sides has a long suit and each side attempts to establish its suit before the other. The defenders have the advantage of the opening lead and the player on lead should normally open his longest suit.

The opening lead
Certain conventions attach to the lead from a long suit. When three honours are held it is usual to lead the top of a SEQUENCE (King from K Q J) or the higher of touching honours (Jack from K J 10), with the exception that the King is led from a combination headed by A K. When only two honours are held the conventional lead is the FOURTH BEST (the 5 from A Q 7 5 2). This is mainly for reasons of COMMUNICATION. For example, suppose a suit is distributed as :

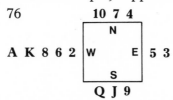

By leading a low card, in this case the 6, West keeps in touch with his partner. As soon as East obtains the lead he can return his second card and the defence will take four tricks.

Sometimes the lead from the long suit will be undesirable for one of these reasons:
1 The opponents have bid your best suit.
2 Partner has bid a suit and you judge that it will be better to play for his hand.
3 Your hand is very poor and lacks ENTRIES. In this case it will be sensible to try to find partner's long suit.

4 The lead of your best suit seems particularly unattractive. With a four-card suit such as K Q x x, A Q x x or A Q J x you may prefer to retain the high cards over the declarer.

When one of these conditions exists you may lead from a SHORT SUIT. From 7,4 or 7,4,2 lead the 7; it will usually be easy for partner to read this as TOP OF NOTHING rather than fourth best from a long suit. But with three cards headed by an honour lead the low card. This saves a trick in numerous situations of the kind shown in *Fig. 77*.

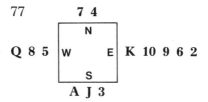

77   **7 4**

Q 8 5   N W E S   **K 10 9 6 2**

A J 3

You can see that if you lead the Queen you give declarer two tricks. If you lead low the King is headed by the Ace and when partner gains the lead he can play the 10 through declarer's J 3.

The race for tricks

Various tactical moves are available to both sides in the race to establish long suits. This is an example of the HOLD-UP—*Fig. 78*.

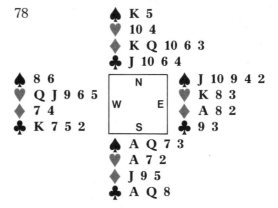

78

     ♠ **K 5**
     ♥ **10 4**
     ♦ **K Q 10 6 3**
     ♣ **J 10 6 4**

♠ **8 6**   ♠ **J 10 9 4 2**
♥ **Q J 9 6 5**   N   ♥ **K 8 3**
♦ **7 4**   W   E   ♦ **A 8 2**
♣ **K 7 5 2**   S   ♣ **9 3**

     ♠ **A Q 7 3**
     ♥ **A 7 2**
     ♦ **J 9 5**
     ♣ **A Q 8**

South opens 1NT on his balanced 17 points. North has only 9 points in high cards, but the five-card suit and the three 10's make the hand worth a raise to 3NT. Note that North does not mention his diamond suit: a simple take-out of Two Diamonds would be a weak response and Three Diamonds would suggest more than 3NT.

Trick 1 West leads the Queen of Hearts, East plays 8 and South 2.

West leads the top card of his BROKEN SEQUENCE. East's play of the 8 is an encouraging SIGNAL; if he had no liking for hearts he would play his lowest card. South could capture this trick with the Ace but refrains from doing so for a reason that will soon appear.

Trick 2 West continues with a low heart to his partner's King and South holds off again.

Trick 3 East plays a third heart, won by South's Ace: Dummy discards a club.

Trick 4 South leads the 9 of diamonds and holds the trick.

South could CASH three top tricks in spades if he wanted to, but this would be bad play for two reasons: it would set up spade winners for the defence and it would remove an entry card from dummy.

Trick 5 South leads a diamond to the 10 and East holds off again.

Trick 6 A third round of diamonds is won by East's Ace. (See *Fig. 79*).

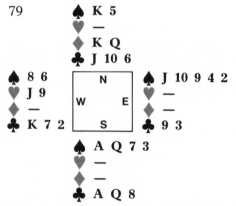

79

♠ K 5
♥ —
♦ K Q
♣ J 10 6

♠ 8 6
♥ J 9
♦ —
♣ K 7 2

♠ J 10 9 4 2
♥ —
♦ —
♣ 9 3

♠ A Q 7 3
♥ —
♦ —
♣ A Q 8

Trick 7 East leads the 9 of clubs and South wins with the Ace.

The point of South's earlier hold-up play is now clear. Unable to lead a heart, East tries to give his partner the lead in clubs. South can see nine tricks, however; he goes up with the Ace of clubs, refusing the finesse.

The rest of the play is straightforward. South crosses to the King of spades, cashes two diamonds, and makes two more spade tricks.

Ducking play

In *Fig. 80* the declarer makes use of ducking play to bring in dummy's long suit.

South opens One Diamond and North responds One Heart. With a balanced 16 and two 10's South rebids 2NT. North has not much to spare but raises to 3NT. It is a borderline contract.

Trick 1 West leads the 4 of spades, East plays the King and South wins with the Ace.

80

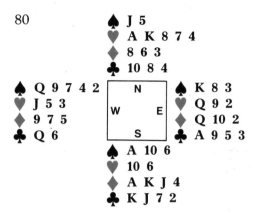

♠ J 5
♥ A K 8 7 4
♦ 8 6 3
♣ 10 8 4

♠ Q 9 7 4 2
♥ J 5 3
♦ 9 7 5
♣ Q 6

♠ K 8 3
♥ Q 9 2
♦ Q 10 2
♣ A 9 5 3

♠ A 10 6
♥ 10 6
♦ A K J 4
♣ K J 7 2

South does not hold off on this occasion because, by playing the Ace on the King, he can be sure of two spade tricks.

Trick 2 South leads the 10 of hearts, plays low from dummy, and loses to East's Queen.

Declarer must hope to bring in dummy's heart suit. It is essential to duck the first round as there are no side entries to the dummy.

Trick 3 East leads the 8 of spades, South and West play low, and the Jack wins.

East follows normal tactics in returning his partner's suit. West can tell from the play that South holds the 10, so he ducks this trick to retain communication with his partner.

Tricks 4–7 Declarer plays off four rounds of hearts from dummy.

Trick 8 A diamond is led and the Jack is finessed. South has made six tricks already and the top diamonds will provide two more. He does not attempt to develop the ninth trick in clubs because he expects the defenders to take the Ace of clubs and three more spades.

When the diamond finesse holds, South plays off the Ace and King. If he has kept all his diamonds he ends up with ten tricks—four hearts, four diamonds and two spades.

Attacking the danger hand

On most hands the declarer needs to develop tricks in two suits and it may be very important to attack the right suit first. In general, it is right to attack the entries of the dangerous hand. The first step, of course, is to decide which is the dangerous opponent (see *Fig. 81*). In *Fig. 81* South opens 1NT on his balanced 15 and North forces with Three Hearts. As he holds honours in every suit and has 4-3-3-3 distribution, South rebids 3NT rather than Four Hearts. This turns out to be a good decision, for in hearts there is a loser in each suit.

81

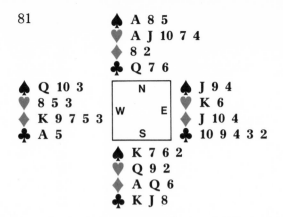

```
                        ♠ A 8 5
                        ♥ A J 10 7 4
                        ♦ 8 2
                        ♣ Q 7 6
   ♠ Q 10 3          ┌─────────┐       ♠ J 9 4
   ♥ 8 5 3           │    N    │       ♥ K 6
   ♦ K 9 7 5 3       │ W     E │       ♦ J 10 4
   ♣ A 5             │    S    │       ♣ 10 9 4 3 2
                     └─────────┘
                        ♠ K 7 6 2
                        ♥ Q 9 2
                        ♦ A Q 6
                        ♣ K J 8
```

West opens his fourth best diamond and East plays the 10 lowest from cards in sequence. South is obliged to win with the Queen. It is clear that most tricks can be developed in hearts, but if the finesse loses and diamonds are cleared South will have only eight quick winners. As soon as clubs are touched, West will win and make the setting tricks in diamonds.

West is the danger hand, so his entries should be attacked first. At trick 2 South must lead the Jack of clubs. Suppose, first, that West wins with the Ace and continues diamonds. South will hold off until the third round and will later take the heart finesse quite safely.

It is more likely that West, hoping to preserve his entry card, will allow the Jack of clubs to hold. South must then turn promptly to hearts. The finesse loses but he has nine safe tricks by way of four hearts, two spades, two diamonds and one club. If South needed two tricks from clubs it would be right to play a second round, but that would be an unnecessary risk here. It would cost him the contract against best defence. West will win the second club and play a low diamond to his partner's Jack. South must hold off and then East unkindly leads a third round of clubs. The King of hearts has not been driven out yet and the defence will take three clubs, a diamond and a heart.

Timing in defence
Needless to say, the declarer does not always prevail. *Fig. 82* is an example of well-timed defence against a part score contract.

South opens One Club, North responds One Diamond and South rebids 1NT. North raises to 2NT but South can do no more.

Trick 1 West leads the 4 of hearts, dummy plays low and East wins with the Queen. As the cards lie on this deal, South would do better

82

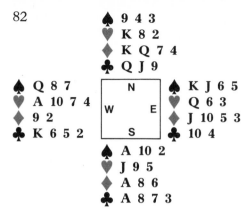

♠ 9 4 3
♥ K 8 2
♦ K Q 7 4
♣ Q J 9

♠ Q 8 7
♥ A 10 7 4
♦ 9 2
♣ K 6 5 2

♠ K J 6 5
♥ Q 6 3
♦ J 10 5 3
♣ 10 4

♠ A 10 2
♥ J 9 5
♦ A 8 6
♣ A 8 7 3

to go up with the King of hearts, but that would not be natural play. East, in turn, must not be too mean to contribute the Queen. To play low would be a crime known as 'finessing against partner'.

Trick 2 East switches to a low spade and West wins with the Queen. East has noted that his partner led the 4 of hearts, dummy holds the 2 and East himself the 3. This means that West, who will have led fourth best, has only a four-card suit. This type of inference is very common and very important. As to continue hearts would set up one extra trick at most, East SWITCHES to a spade. (To play a second round of hearts would not necessarily be fatal on this hand, but the switch up to dummy's weakness is certainly better play.)

Trick 3 West returns a spade and East's Jack holds the trick.

Placing his partner with K J x x or possibly A x x x, West is happy to continue spades. East's K J are now EQUALS, as the Queen has been played. While it is correct to *lead* the higher of touching cards it is correct to *play* the lower. South holds off again.

Trick 4 East leads the 6 of hearts to West's Ace. East could establish the thirteenth spade but has no side entry. With two spade tricks in the bag he reverts to his partner's original suit. West now takes the Ace, intending to CLEAR the suit by playing a third round.

Trick 5 The third heart is won by dummy's King.

Trick 6 South finesses the Jack of clubs, losing to West's King.

Trick 7 West cashes the 10 of hearts and South is one down, losing two spades, three hearts and one club.

It is not difficult to see that against a wooden defence South would have made this contract. Suppose that the defenders begin with three rounds of hearts. South takes the club finesse, West wins, cashes the thirteenth heart and switches to a spade. Now declarer will make at least three clubs, three diamonds, one heart and one spade.

THE PLAY IN A
SUIT CONTRACT

At no-trumps the time element is so important that the defenders will cheerfully lead away from 'dangerous' combinations such as AQxxx, KJxxx, or Jxxxx, where the lead is likely to cost an early trick. In a trump contract there is not as a rule the same advantage in establishing long suits. The defenders therefore pay more heed to the element of safety.

The opening lead
The conventional lead from most honour sequences is the same as against no-trumps, with these exceptions:
From K Q and others lead the King, not fourth best.
From Q J and others lead the Queen.
From Ace and others lead the Ace (but still the King from AK).

In each case you seek to avoid giving the declarer a cheap trick. One reason for not UNDERLEADING an Ace is that declarer may have a singleton in one hand, the King in the other, and so not lose any trick in the suit at all.

Leads from weak suits are much more common against a trump contract than against no-trumps. The lead from a singleton or doubleton gives nothing away and has the further advantage that it may lead to a ruff.

A lead of the trump suit itself is usually safe enough but tends to be helpful to the declarer. The time to lead trumps is when you can judge from the bidding that declarer has found a good fit and is likely to make his trumps separately.

The opening lead against a suit contract is a tactical problem which cannot be divorced from the bidding and the make-up of the leader's hand. The whole picture will become clearer as we study the different forms of play in trump contracts.

Delaying trump leads for a discard
The declarer in a suit contract should always ask himself at an early

stage whether or not he should draw trumps. It is always right to draw trumps unless there is a clearly defined reason not to. Such a reason often exists, to be sure, but it is wise to form a habit and note the exceptions. In this first example *Fig. 83* the declarer needs to establish an early discard and must attack a side suit first.

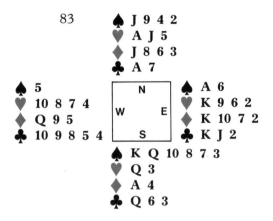

83

```
            ♠ J 9 4 2
            ♥ A J 5
            ♦ J 8 6 3
            ♣ A 7
♠ 5                      ♠ A 6
♥ 10 8 7 4        N      ♥ K 9 6 2
♦ Q 9 5       W     E    ♦ K 10 7 2
♣ 10 9 8 5 4      S      ♣ K J 2
            ♠ K Q 10 8 7 3
            ♥ Q 3
            ♦ A 4
            ♣ Q 6 3
```

South opens One Spade and North raises to Three Spades. South has not much in hand in terms of points, but with a six-card suit he will certainly try for game in spades.

The 10 of clubs is a safe and mildly constructive lead. From South's point of view West may have led away from the King of clubs and in most circumstances it would be right to let the lead run up to the King. Can you see why (apart from the lie of the cards) that would be wrong here?

It is a matter of TEMPO. South is threatened with the possible loss of a trick in each suit. He can, however, dispose of his diamond loser on dummy's Jack of hearts so long as he acts quickly.

The proper play is to go up with the Ace of clubs and lead a low heart, letting the opponents make the King. Say that they cash the King of clubs and switch to a diamond: you go up with the Ace and hastily discard a diamond on the third round of hearts. Only then do you play trumps. Barring accidents such as a 6–2 division of hearts you make Four Spades for the loss of one spade, one heart and one club.

Taking ruffs in dummy

The commonest reason for not drawing trumps early on is that declarer needs to take ruffs in dummy. Example *84* also illustrates the principle that what is wrong for declarer (in this instance, to draw trumps) is likely to be right for the defenders.

84

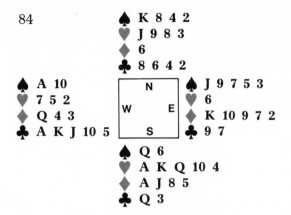

South opens One Heart and West overcalls with Two Clubs. North produces a minimum raise to Two Hearts and this encourages South to go for game in Four Hearts.

West leads the King of clubs and East, holding a doubleton, drops the 9. This is the commencement of a PETER, or ECHO. With three low cards East would play the lowest; when he plays HIGH-LOW, he tells his partner he has a doubleton and invites a continuation. West continues with the Ace of clubs and East plays the 7, completing his peter.

Misguidedly, as it turns out, West plays a third round of clubs. East discards a spade and South ruffs. Declarer can easily draw trumps, but if he does so he will be left with losing diamonds. The obvious continuation is Ace of diamonds, followed by a diamond ruff.

South needs to establish a spade trick sooner or later and it is good technique to play this suit at once. A low spade is headed by the Queen and Ace. Somewhat belatedly, West leads a trump. South's 10 wins and the cards shown in *Fig. 85* are left.

85

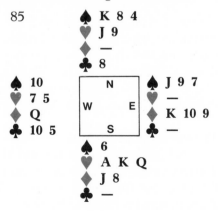

It is simple now to cash the King of spades and CROSS-RUFF the remainder of the hand, making the five trumps separately.

As the reader will have noted, West's defence was poor. The singleton diamond in dummy should have warned him to lead trumps as soon as possible. A trump at trick 2 was obvious and even at trick 3 a heart would have created a problem. Declarer can contrive to ruff all his diamonds but meanwhile he has not cleared his trick in spades.

Establishing a suit in dummy

One of the most valuable uses of the trump suit is to establish a side suit. In example *86* trumps are not drawn immediately because in the course of going from hand to hand declarer needs to use the trumps suit for entries.

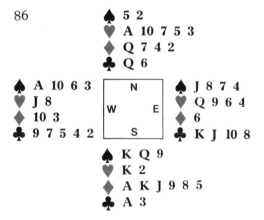

86

```
                ♠ 5 2
                ♥ A 10 7 5 3
                ♦ Q 7 4 2
                ♣ Q 6
♠ A 10 6 3      ┌─────────┐      ♠ J 8 7 4
♥ J 8           │    N    │      ♥ Q 9 6 4
♦ 10 3          │ W     E │      ♦ 6
♣ 9 7 5 4 2     │    S    │      ♣ K J 10 8
                └─────────┘
                ♠ K Q 9
                ♥ K 2
                ♦ A K J 9 8 5
                ♣ A 3
```

With East-West silent the bidding goes:

South	North
2 ♦	2 ♥
3 ♦	4 ♦
4NT	5 ♦
6 ♦	No

South uses the Blackwood convention to discover how many Aces his partner holds. Finding that an Ace is missing he stops in a small slam.

West must consider whether to lead the Ace of spades. It is not wrong in general to lead an Ace against a slam contract, but here West would be leading up to the strong hand, there is no prospect of finding partner with a second Ace, and South almost surely holds second-round control of spades. You will note that the Ace of spades would in fact be a disastrous lead, enabling South to discard a losing club from dummy on the third round of spades.

As there is nothing to recommend a diamond or a heart, West leads the 4 of clubs. South puts up dummy's Queen without much hope, East plays the King and South must win as otherwise he will lose a club and a spade at once.

There is a top loser in spades and South must somehow dispose of his second club. The plan must be to establish at least one extra trick in hearts. This can be done if the suit is breaking not worse than 4–2, but there may be an entry problem and South must play carefully. The correct sequence is as follows:

Trick 1 Ace of clubs.

Trick 2 Ace of diamonds. South can afford one high trump at this point, but not more.

Tricks 3–4 King and Ace of hearts.

Trick 5 A low heart from dummy, ruffed with the Jack of diamonds. The 5 of diamonds will be needed later for entry to dummy, and furthermore South must not allow West to overruff.

Trick 6 Unblocking again, South leads the 9 of diamonds to dummy's Queen.

Trick 7 A fourth round of hearts is ruffed by the 8. The position is now as illustrated in *Fig. 87*.

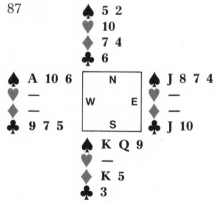

Trick 8 South leads the 5 of diamonds to dummy's 7.

Trick 9 The 10 of hearts is led and South discards the 3 of clubs.

Declarer loses a trick to the Ace of spades now, but there is a trump in dummy for the third round of spades.

There were two critical moves in the play. South had to attack hearts after just one round of trumps and he had to unblock three times to preserve his 5 of diamonds.

The correct play is easier to find than you may think. As South needs to establish a long heart he must assume that both opponents will follow to the King and Ace, so there is no real risk in playing the suit before drawing the last trump. As for the 5 of diamonds, a good player, even if half asleep, would ruff high, keeping the entry situation fluid. That sort of play soon becomes automatic.

The fight for trump control

In the examples so far the declarer has not been embarrassed by any shortage of trumps. He has always had enough trumps to control the play. Many hands resolve themselves into a battle for trump control. That is what happens on the following deal in *Fig. 88*.

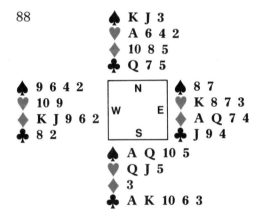

88

	♠ K J 3	
	♥ A 6 4 2	
	♦ 10 8 5	
	♣ Q 7 5	

♠ 9 6 4 2		♠ 8 7
♥ 10 9	N	♥ K 8 7 3
♦ K J 9 6 2	W E	♦ A Q 7 4
♣ 8 2	S	♣ J 9 4

	♠ A Q 10 5	
	♥ Q J 5	
	♦ 3	
	♣ A K 10 6 3	

North-South, with their eyes open, contract for Four Spades though holding only seven trumps, divided 4-3. A combined holding of 4-4 in a major is very satisfactory, for declarer can ruff twice or three times in one hand, then draw trumps with the other. A combined 4-3 is more delicate, especially when the long trump hand is the first to ruff.

West, holding four trumps and expecting South to hold the same number, decides to play a FORCING GAME. That is to say, he aims to weaken the declarer's trump holding by forcing him to ruff. To this end, he leads his long suit, choosing the 6 of diamonds. East wins with the Ace and returns the 4, his original fourth best.

A ham-handed declarer would ruff and attempt to pull the trumps in three rounds. This would leave West with the master trump and three good diamonds.

Slightly better, after ruffing the second round of diamonds, is to take the heart finesse. East wins and, we will say, plays another round of diamonds, though a trump would be better. South ruffs with the Queen of spades, draws three rounds of trumps, and makes one more trick than before.

On this deal South can escape his troubles by the simple expedient of discarding two hearts on the second and third rounds of diamonds. If the defenders lead a fourth round dummy can 'take the force' and declarer's trump holding remains intact. He can draw all the trumps and make game with five spades and either five clubs or four clubs and one heart.

Dummy reversal

When a golfer has a long putt to negotiate he will generally study it from both ends. This is a sound idea in any suit contract where the trumps are more or less evenly divided between declarer and dummy. Hands, like faces, tend to look different when viewed upside down.

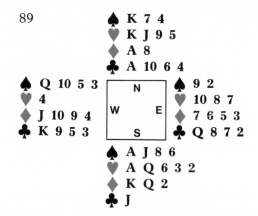

In *Fig. 89* North-South reach a grand slam as follows:

South	North
1 ♥	3 ♣[1]
3 ♠	4 ♥[2]
4NT[3]	5 ♥[4]
6 ♦[5]	6 ♠[6]
7 ♥	

[1]Too strong for a direct raise to Four Hearts, North forces to game.

[2]The spade bid improves the look of North's hand but he has already expressed his values by forcing and a simple return to hearts is enough at this point.

69

³Blackwood, asking for Aces.

⁴Showing two Aces.

⁵South might bid 5NT at this point, asking for Kings, but it will not help him greatly to discover that his partner has either one or two Kings. By bidding a new suit at the Six level South says: 'We certainly hold all the first-round controls and there is no worry about diamonds. If you have undisclosed values there should be a grand slam'.

North, whose previous Four Hearts was conservative, is glad of the chance to catch up. He chooses Six Spades because it is possible that his partner may want to play in no-trumps when he learns about the King of spades.

A trump is often a good lead against a grand slam, but with a singleton there is the slight danger that you may be killing partner's Qxx or J 10xx. West has a sound choice in the Jack of diamonds.

How would you plan the play as South? Apart from the simple spade finesse, one possibility is to draw trumps in three rounds, discard a spade from dummy on the third round of diamonds, then play King of spades, Ace of spades, and a third spade which you ruff. This line will succeed if the Queen of spades comes down in three rounds.

It is slightly better to defer trump leads, retaining the possibility to ruff two spades in dummy. You discard a spade on the third diamond as before, then play King of spades, Ace of spades and a low spade. If West shows out on this trick you can ruff low and organise to ruff a second spade later. As the cards lie, West follows to the third spade and for temporary safety you ruff with the Jack of hearts. East shows void and now the contract cannot be made, for if you ruff high again you will lose a trump trick to East's 10-8-7 and if you ruff low you will be overruffed.

After these two false tries can you see a better line? Imagine for a moment that you are sitting in the North seat. Now the play appears quite simple. Your possible spade loser will go away on the Queen of diamonds and you should be able to ruff the three losing clubs. This is the exact sequence of play:

Trick 1 Win the diamond in the South hand as you want to retain entries to dummy.

Tricks 2–3 Lead a club to the Ace and ruff a club. You must begin this process at once.

Tricks 4–5 Ace of hearts and a heart to the King. If trumps are 2-2

Above: Transformation Cards with Original Slip-case. *Centre left:* Miniature Cards, One with Original Straw Case. *Centre right:* Cards from a Pack Celebrating Queen Victoria's Diamond Jubilee. *Below left:* Viennese Cards Illustrating Scenes from Schiller and Körner. *Below right:* Queen and Jack, with Case, from a Piquet Pack

the hand is lay-down, so you must not take unnecessary risks.

Tricks 6–8 You ruff another club, enter dummy with Ace of diamonds and ruff the fourth club with your last trump, the Queen.

Trick 9 You cross to the King of spades.

Trick 10 You draw the outstanding trump with the Jack of hearts, discarding a spade from hand. When you use dummy's trumps in this way to extract the enemy's trumps you are said to REVERSE THE DUMMY.

Tricks 11–13 are taken by dummy's last trump, the Ace of spades and the Queen of diamonds.

Do you wonder where the extra trick has come from? The answer is that by ruffing three clubs in your own hand you have extended the trick-winning power of the trump suit to seven–four in dummy plus three in your own hand. You could not safely achieve the same result by ruffing twice in dummy, because of the danger of an overruff.

The examples in these last two chapters have covered a variety of tactical situations and we hope they have given you some insight into the character of this wonderful game. If you ask 'Where do I go from here?' the first answer is 'Practise' and the second 'Practise with better players'. When you have some experience, read a book that describes a complete system of bidding. Join a bridge club– you won't find that the players are all experts, by any means. As soon as you dare, play competitive bridge. Have a go!

Indian Playing Cards with Lacquered Box

ABOUT THE CARDS

The modern card player might be forgiven for supposing that cards were designed solely for the purpose of playing card games and that they follow a standard pattern—apart, of course, from special packs intended for such games as Happy Families. Both assumptions, seen in historical perspective, would be wrong. Like stamps, cards have always been the playground of artists, and like cigarette cards they have often been adapted to educational, geographical, political and similar purposes. The illustrations in this book give some idea of their endless variety.

Where cards began is not known for certain. It is quite likely that they developed from a kind of paper money used in China, although there is a wide difference between Eastern and Western playing cards. Card games appear to have been played in Europe since the latter part of the 14th century. The earliest reference is in a manuscript of 1377, written by a monk in a Swiss monastery and preserved in the British Museum. Italy, Spain, Germany and France were the countries most active in the manufacture and design of playing cards. The English were always good customers but it was not until 1628 that a royal charter was granted to the Worshipful Company of Makers of Playing Cards.

The playing of cards has never enjoyed much favour from Authority, except as a source of revenue. Henry VIII attempted to divert his subjects from card playing to archery. In a sense the struggle still goes on, with a government body officiously controlling establishments where games of chance are played. The Church was an early opponent of cards, partly because of the gambling element, partly because of the association with fortune-telling. In 1423 St. Bernadine of Sienna denounced playing cards as the invention of the devil. Another view is that the devil is an invention of luckless card players!

Modern Playing Cards

The vigorous and attractive design of modern cards, seen on the jacket photograph, is derived from an artist's impression of costumes worn at the French court in the 14th century. The double ends and corner pips are a later development. In all other respects the design is very similar to that of a pack made at Rouen in 1675.

Jeu des Nouveaux Cris de Paris

'Baskets! Water! Vegetables! Chickweed!' The pack of 32 cards illustrated on page 17, together with its original cardboard case, shows the colourful costumes and cheerful countenances of trades-men calling their wares in the Paris of 1770.

Cards from Vienna

The two sets illustrated on page 18 are by Piatnik and Sohne of Vienna, a firm still active in the production of new designs. One of the packs illustrated is dated 1845 and the other, varying only slightly in pattern, somewhat later.

Astronomy Cards

The cards shown on page 35, photographed with their original slip-case, were used in the court game of Astronomy. One of the purposes of the game is expressed in the final paragraph of the Explanation which accompanied the cards: 'The mind is thus familiarised with the heavenly bodies while engaged in the usual Games in which cards are employed, and instruction in the sublime science of Astronomy combined with a pleasing and elegant amusement'.

Chinese Chungking Playing Cards

The cards illustrated opposite page 36 are unmistakably of Chinese design. They are inscribed on oiled paper and are a development of paper money. The complete pack contains 111 cards.

Cartes Très Fines

The miscellany of beautiful cards on page 53 contains: Queen of clubs and Ace of hearts from an English pack of 1780; the 10 and 2 from a pack by Grimaud of Paris; 1 and 11 made in Genova, Italy for use in Spain; King and Queen of diamonds, and remaining cards fanned out, from a Piquet pack made in Paris about 1816, described as *Cartes très fines*.

Political, Heraldic and Geographical Cards

Cards of political, heraldic and geographical import are illustrated on page 54. The Dutch cards fitting into their original leather case and the two below are from a pack containing satirical comment on the South Sea Bubble crisis of 1720. The wording beneath the cockerel reads: 'These fine fashionable cards were made at Scotch-cock-town by Lawrens Bumbarist (the Humbug) at (the sign of) the Rooting Dream goldmine digger'.

At the top left are specimens of 17th century heraldry cards.

Those cards which are marked 'Angleterre' and 'Ecosse' are from a French pack of the 17th century which served as an educational aid to the geography of England, Scotland, Ireland and Holland.

The Queen of spades and the 4 of hearts are 18th century French, adapted from Viennese designs.

Transformation and Celebration Cards

The cards at the top of page 71 are of a type known as 'transformation' where the suit symbols are incorporated into the design: a form of pictorial pun. The popinjay looking into the mirror is saying, 'I think this attitude will do'. The quotes on the 4 of hearts are: 'Madam I am eternally yours', answered by 'Are you in earnest Sir?' and 'Angels are painted fair to look like you' with the reply 'Spare my blushes'.

On the right can be seen the front and back of cards printed by Goodall to mark Queen Victoria's diamond jubilee.

Centre left illustrates a miniature pack of 36 cards with the German suits of Hearts, Acorns, Bells and Leaves. Next to it is another miniature pack with its own exquisite straw case.

The 7 of clubs and 5 of hearts, shown at the bottom left, are Viennese and illustrate two scenes from Schiller and Körner.

The Queen of diamonds and Jack of clubs, with their original slip-case, are from a Piquet pack made in Frankfurt.

Indian Playing Cards

The superb hand-painted cards illustrated on page 72 are examples of 18th century Hindustani craftsmanship. A pack consisted of 10 suits, with 12 cards in each suit. In all suits the King is mounted on an elephant and the Vizier or second Honour is on horseback. The oblong wooden box is decorated with paint and lacquered in rich colours and gold.

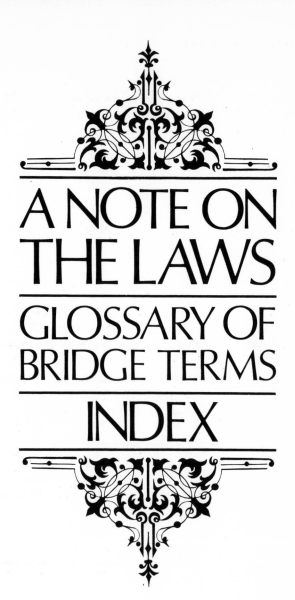

A NOTE ON
THE LAWS

GLOSSARY OF
BRIDGE TERMS

INDEX

A NOTE ON THE LAWS

There is an official code of Laws for bridge, determined by an international body. The complete code is highly complicated and only professional tournament directors would claim to know all the regulations by heart. Players learning the game are unlikely to be tigers for exacting every penalty but it is important to realise that it is good etiquette to follow the provisions of the Laws. As the book has it, 'The Laws are designed to define correct procedure and to provide an adequate remedy in all cases where a player accidentally, carelessly or inadvertently disturbs the proper course of the game, or gains an unintentional but nevertheless unfair advantage. An offending player should be ready to pay a prescribed penalty graciously.'

We summarise below the penalties for the commonest infringements. Note that this is *only* a summary and a general guide for friendly games.

The Auction Period

Call out of turn
A call out of turn is condoned if the next player speaks before drawing attention to the irregularity. Otherwise, the bidding reverts to the player whose proper turn it was. The penalty depends on the timing and nature of the call.

[1] If it was a pass before any bid had been made, or a pass when it was the turn of the right-hand opponent to speak, the only penalty is that the player must pass at his turn.

[2] If it was a pass in any other circumstances, the offender must pass throughout and his partner may not double or redouble at this turn.

[3] If a player makes a positive bid out of turn his partner is silenced for the rest of the auction.

Insufficient bid

If a player makes a bid that is insufficient to overcall the previous bid he must amend in one of the following ways:

[1]By making the lowest sufficient call in the same denomination – e.g. by amending an insufficient bid of Two Hearts to whatever number of hearts is required. NO PENALTY.

[2]By passing. PENALTY: the offender's partner must pass throughout.

[3]By substituting any other sufficient bid (not a double or redouble). PENALTY: the offender's partner must pass throughout.

Note: In some of the cases described above there is also a lead penalty should the non-offending side obtain the contract. In a friendly game it is sufficient that the player who leads should not take advantage of any information improperly obtained.

The Playing Period

Penalty card

If a card is accidentally dropped face upwards by a defender, or is exposed in the commission of an irregularity such as a lead out of turn, it may be treated as a penalty card. Such card must be left face upwards on the table and must be played at the first opportunity. There is no penalty for the exposure of a card by the declarer and a card belonging to dummy never becomes a penalty card.

Lead out of turn

a By a defender. Declarer may accept the lead out of turn; if it was the opening lead, dummy is spread and plays last to the first trick. Alternatively, declarer may treat the card led out of turn as a penalty card. Or declarer may allow the card to be picked up and may forbid or require the partner to lead that suit.

b By declarer or dummy. Declarer may not retract the card wrongly led unless requested to do so. If so requested he must if possible lead the same suit from the correct hand.

Revoke

A revoke may be corrected and a correct card substituted up to the moment at which the offender or his partner has led or played to the next trick. The revoke card, if played by a defender, becomes a penalty card. A card played by the non-offending side after the revoke may be withdrawn.

A revoke becomes established when the offender or his partner leads or plays to the subsequent trick. PENALTY: up to two tricks are transferred to the non-offending side and count exactly as though won in play; BUT tricks won previously to the revoke cannot be so transferred and there is no additional penalty for a second revoke in the same suit by the same player.

Claims and concessions

If a declarer shows his hand or claims a number of tricks he may be required to make a full statement of how he intends to play. Thereafter he may not finesse and may be required to draw or not to draw an outstanding trump that he may have forgotten.

If a defender shows his cards or makes a claim, declarer may treat the remaining cards of the other defender as penalty cards.

Dummy's rights

Dummy is entitled to warn his partner against committing an irregularity or to draw attention to an opponent's irregularity; but dummy forfeits his rights if he looks at another player's hand.

SCORING TABLE

Score when an undoubled contract is made

The trick score is entered below the line at the following rate:

Spades or hearts	30 per trick
Diamonds or clubs	20 per trick
No-trumps	40 for first trick, 30 for each subsequent trick.

Overtricks are entered above the line at the same rate (but when game has been scored the result may be entered as a single figure, e.g. 3NT bid and Four made may be entered as 130).

A score of 100 below the line wins a game and a line is drawn beneath it. There is no bonus for a single game, but see below **Bonus for rubber.**

Score when a doubled or redoubled contract is made

The trick score is multiplied by two when the contract has been doubled, by four when it has been redoubled. There is a bonus of 50, additional to all other scores, when any doubled or redoubled contract is made. Overtricks are scored at the following rate:

	Not vulnerable	Vulnerable
Doubled	100 per trick	200 per trick
Redoubled	200 per trick	400 per trick

Penalties when a contract is defeated

	Not vulnerable	Vulnerable
Undoubled	50 per trick	100 per trick
Doubled	100 for the first trick, 200 for each subsequent trick	200 for the first trick, 300 for each subsequent trick
Redoubled	Twice the above	Twice the above

Bonus for honours

For four honours in the trump suit held by any player	100
For five honours in the trump suit held by any player	150
For four Aces at no-trumps held by any player	150

Bonuses for slam

	Not vulnerable	Vulnerable
Small slam	500	750
Grand slam	1000	1500

Bonus for rubber

When the rubber is won in two games	700
When the rubber is won by two games to one	500

Bonus in unfinished rubber

For a side that is a game ahead	300
For a part score in an unfinished game	50

GLOSSARY OF BRIDGE TERMS

Above the Line	All scores except for tricks bid and made are entered above the line on the score-sheet.
Approach Bid	Style of bidding a short suit by way of approach.
Auction	The bidding period.
Below the Line	Scores for tricks bid and made are entered below the line on the score-sheet.
Bid	Call whereby the player undertakes to win tricks in a specified contract.
Call	Any bid, double, redouble or pass.
Cash	Play off an established winner.
Contract	The final bid of the auction, which may be doubled or redoubled, determines the contract.
Control	Holding such as Ace, King, void or singleton that will enable the player to win the first or second round.
Convention	Agreement to attach a particular meaning to a bid or play.
Cue-bid	Bid to show a control; also, overcall in a suit bid by the opponents.
Cut	Division of the pack when presented to the dealer.
Declarer	Player who first mentioned the denomination in which the final contract is played.
Defender	Player whose opponents have opened the bidding; in play, opponent of the declarer.
Denomination	Nature of contract, either suit or no-trumps.
Discard	Play of a card not of the suit led and not a trump.
Double	Call that increases the penalties if a contract is not made or the bonus if it is made.
Doubleton	The holding of two cards in a suit.
Draw	To play off; in the trump suit, to extract.
Duck	Play of a low card for tactical reasons.
Dummy	Partner of the declarer; his hand, which is exposed after the opening lead.
Echo	High-low signal in defence.
Entry	Card that affords entry to a player's hand.

84

Finesse	Attempt to win a trick with a card that is not the highest.
Follow Suit	Play a card of the suit led.
Force	Bid that requires partner to respond; in play, attempt to shorten the declarer's trump holding.
Game	A score of 100 or more below the line wins a game.
Honour	An Ace, King, Queen, Jack or Ten.
Hold-up	Refusal to part with a winning card.
Intermediate	Valuable card such as 8, 9 or 10.
Jump Bid	Bid higher than necessary to overcall the previous bid.
Lead	The first card played to a trick.
Long Card	Established low-card winner.
Major Suit	Spades or hearts.
Minor Suit	Diamonds or clubs.
Negative Response	Response denying certain values.
No-trumps	Contract in which there is no trump suit.
Odd Tricks	Tricks won by declarer in excess of six.
Open	Make the first bid or, in play, the first lead.
Overcall	Bid by a defender over an opponent's opening.
Overtricks	Tricks in excess of contract.
Part Score	Contract for less than game.
Pass	Call meaning that the player does not wish to bid, double or redouble.
Penalty	Points lost by a side that has failed to make a contract.
Penalty Pass	Pass that converts a take-out double into a penalty double.
Peter	High-low signal in defence.
Point Count	Assessment of high cards in terms of points.
Positive Response	Response promising certain values.
Raise	Support of partner's bid.
Redouble	Call that increases penalties or bonuses after a contract has been doubled.
Re-open	To bid or double in last position when the bidding would otherwise have ended.
Respond	To reply to partner's opening bid.
Revoke	Fail to follow suit when able to do so.
Rubber	A side that has won two games wins the rubber.
Ruff	To play a trump when a side suit has been led.
Sacrifice	Bid that invites a penalty to save a game or part score.
Sequence	Run of adjacent or nearly adjacent cards.
Side Suit	Suit other than the trump suit.
Sign-off	Bid that warns partner to pass.
Singleton	A holding of one card in a suit.
Slam	Contract to make twelve tricks, a small slam, or thirteen tricks, a grand slam.
System	Complete bidding method.
Take-out Double	Double that invites partner to bid.
Tempo	Unit of time in the play.

Trick   The lead and the three cards that follow make up a trick.

Trump   Suit named in the contract that wins over any other suit; a card of that suit; to play such a card when another suit has been led.

Unblock   Play of an unnecessarily high card for reasons of entry.

Undertrick   Tricks whereby declarer falls short of his contract.

Void   A holding of no cards in a suit.

Vulnerable   State of pair that has won a game.

INDEX